sauvignon
blanc

sauvignon
blanc

a complete guide to the grape
and the wines it produces

MITCHELL BEAZLEY

susy atkins

sauvignon blanc

by susy atkins

First published in Great Britain in 2003
by Mitchell Beazley, an imprint of Octopus
Publishing Group Limited, 2–4 Heron Quays,
London E14 4JP.

A CIP catalogue record for this book is
available from the British Library.

ISBN: 1 84000 687 0

The author and publishers will be grateful
for any information which will assist them
in keeping future editions up to date.
Although all reasonable care has been taken
in the preparation of this book, neither
the publishers nor the author can accept
any liability for any consequences arising
from the use thereof, or the information
contained therein.

Commissioning editor   Hilary Lumsden
Executive art editor   Yasia Williams
Managing editor   Emma Rice
Design   Nicky Collings
Editor   Jamie Ambrose
Production   Alexis Coogan
Index   John Noble

Mitchell Beazley would like to thank the staff at
Oddbins in Camden High Street, London for their
help with the photography.

Typeset in RotisSansSerif

Printed and bound by
Toppan Printing Company in China

Picture acknowledgements
1, 2-3, 5 Octopus Publishing Group/Alan
Williams; 6-7 Octopus Publishing Group/Adrian
Lander; 12-13 Scope/Jacques Guillard; 14-15
Scope/Jean-luc Barde; 16-17 Corbis/Jim
Zuckerman; 19 Octopus Publishing Group/Alan
Williams; 20-21 Octopus Publishing Group/David
Harrison; 22-23 Janet Price; 24-25, 26 Octopus
Publishing Group/Alan Williams; 28-29, 30-31
Janet Price; 33, 34 Octopus Publishing Group/
Alan Williams; 36-37 Adrian Lander/Stok-Yard;
38-39 Root Stock/Hendrik Holler; 40, 43 Octopus
Publishing Group/Alan Williams; 44-45 Janet
Price; 47 Patrick Eagar; 48-49 Root Stock/Hendrik
Holler; 51, 52, 54, 55, 56-57, 58-59, 60-61, 62-
63 Octopus Publishing Group/Alan Williams.

contents

introduction   6

the sauvignon look   8

where sauvignon lives & why   10

sauvignon in good hands   12

sauvignon blends   14

how sauvignon grew up   16

what will become of sauvignon?   18

the countries   20

france   22

italy   28

spain   30

central & eastern europe   32

the rest of europe   34

australia   36

new zealand   38

north america   44

south america   46

south africa   48

buying, storing, & serving   52

quality vs price   54

other wines to try   56

when to serve   58

how to serve   60

what to serve with   62

index   64

introduction

Lots of people are mightily bored with drinking rich, oaky Chardonnay all the time. Of course, they could turn to Riesling, but it's still unfashionable in some quarters. They could turn to New World Semillon or to peachy, fat Viognier, but if they want a serious change – a drier, crisper, leaner style of wine – then Sauvignon Blanc is the obvious choice.

Examine a bunch of Sauvignon Blanc grapes. One of the first things you'll notice is that Sauvignon is not highly coloured. These grapes harbour a relatively low level of pigment, which is why any wines made from them tend to be pale and straw-coloured, rather than yellow-gold like many Chardonnays.

the sauvignon look

Skin

The skin of Sauvignon Blanc grapes is relatively thin, which means it is easily attacked by "noble rot", the *Botrytis cinerea* fungus that shrivels the grape while it's still on the vine. Sounds horrible? It looks it, too, but this benevolent rot concentrates the sweet juice of ripe, mature grapes, while adding some attractive nuances (*see* pages 25-7).

Pulp

Sauvignon Blanc's pulp (and skin) contains flavour or aroma compounds which are described by scientists as methoxypyrazines. These give a particularly herbaceous, green-grassy, even gooseberry and asparagus character to wine made from Sauvignon grapes. The variety is an early ripener, and its acidity levels remain relatively high.

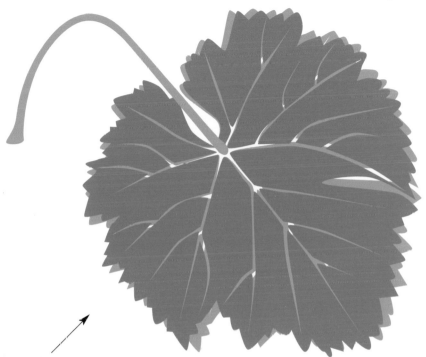

Leaf

This is a vine that likes to grow with abandon – judicious winemakers are careful to limit its vigour. The result is good-quality, ripe grapes exposed to the sun and air, rather than a mass of shoots and leaves, with the fruit hidden in the shade. Cutting back the foliage to reveal the grapes contributes towards the production of high-quality wines.

Bunch (*see* page 6)

Sauvignon is a late-budding vine and an early ripener. The ripeness levels of the grapes need watching carefully. Too little sun, and an over-herbaceous, raw grassiness is evident in the wine; but give it too much heat, and the intensity of fruit flavour and aroma might be lost.

If you want Sauvignon that's aromatic and crisp, with plenty of that vibrant fruity character, then it definitely doesn't pay to cook the grapes. This variety likes the sun – but not too-hot weather. A long, cool, bright ripening season is perfect.

where sauvignon lives & why

This is why Sauvignon is at its best in the cool, breezy, sunny vineyards of Marlborough, on New Zealand's South Island. The long growing and ripening season here, plus a dip in temperature at night, mean that the fruity ripeness is coaxed out of the vine, while high acidity is retained for that essential zesty freshness. In good years, that is.

Over in the grape's other stronghold, the Loire Valley, the weather is on the cooler side, too. This is where the best French examples arise. Further south, in the Languedoc, winemakers struggle more with the heat in the vineyards and often lose that crucial mouthwatering tingle.

It's the same story in other parts of the winemaking globe; where the vineyards are cooler than average, the more elegant, minerally Sauvignons will be found. Thus it is northeast Italy, rather than the south and Sicily, that makes Sauvignon, while down under in Australia, the Adelaide Hills and Tasmania are the most agreeable areas.

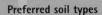

Preferred soil types

Premium Sauvignon Blanc often comes from stony-soiled vineyards, especially limestone-rich ones such as those found in Sancerre and Pouilly-Fumé in the Loire. The limestone vineyard sites produce wines which have a marked mineral-and-chalk, even smoky character (*see* pages 22-4).

Marlborough has produced some of its best Sauvignons from extremely difficult, stony vineyards that make the vines struggle to yield a relatively small, concentrated crop. The Robertson region of South Africa is another place where limestone and rocky terrain pushes Sauvignon into making some of its most expressive, characterful wines.

It's easy to make a bland, fairly fresh, everyday white out of Sauvignon – and many wineries do just that. But creating mediocre, forgettable Sauvignon is to miss the point of this grape entirely. Sauvignon Blanc should be memorable: either for its nervy, spine-tingling elegance, purity, and crispness (think Loire Valley), or for its explosion of rich aroma, and lip-smacking green fruit, asparagus, and tomato leaf (New Zealand).

sauvignon in good hands

There are enough white grapes, such as Ugni Blanc and Müller-Thurgau, that *can't* make exciting wine, so it seems absurd not to squeeze a thrill out of Sauvignon, which can! Many fine examples of this wine do hit a neat balance between the two characters described above, but there's never, ever an excuse for a boring glass of Sauvignon.

Yet that's what you'll get if the grapes that made your wine were overcropped (*i.e.* from high-yielding vines), and therefore dilute and lacking personality. Top winemakers always work with vines that produce low yields of grapes, perhaps because the soil is rocky and hard, or perhaps because the vines are especially old. This fruit has more concentrated flavours, which leads to wine with more intensity and which displays more of the varietal character of Sauvignon Blanc - exactly what is needed in this age of identikit white wines! And they are careful to avoid under-ripeness, which can show up in a wine as an unpleasantly lean, raw capsicum character, like chewing on a raw green bean – not nice at all. Cutting back the leaves to allow the sun in and waiting until the right moment to pick is the obvious solution here. Conversely, Sauvignon that is too ripe can be a disappointment, as it lacks the true character of the variety and tastes flabby.

Some winemakers favour oaked Sauvignon Blanc, which can work (in the case of some fine white Bordeaux), but can also end up being somewhat sweet and characterless in other cases (poor California wine). Most go-ahead producers working today are trying to emphasize the dry, racy, unoaked appeal of Sauvignon – partly, I'm sure, because they want to show a direct contrast with soft, rounded, often oaky Chardonnay.

As always with oak-fermented and oak-aged wines, the best examples of barrel-aged Sauvignon show a fine balance. The oak should enhance rather than overpower the fruit, and this is especially important in the case of mouthwatering, crisp Sauvignon, the flavours of which can clash with too much woody vanilla and spice.

Keeping the fresh flavours in Sauvignon is crucial. The use of modern winemaking techniques, such as controlled cool fermentation and the use of hygenic stainless steel tanks, means you are much more likely to come across refreshing, tangily crisp wines than ever before.

Go to a wine shop, ask the manager to point to any bottles that contain Sauvignon and you'll find the majority are unblended: they're one hundred per cent Sauvignon Blanc. Or rather, that's what the labels say. In reality, *most* bottles labelled "Sauvignon Blanc" contain no other grape variety (and this is true of the Loire greats, too), but a few of them might have a little Sémillon tucked away in there to round out the blend and add some soft ripeness to our Sauvignon's sometimes lean and stalky nature. For example, the classic label, Cloudy Bay, generally has a little Semillon (no "é") added to its Sauvignon. Just a smidgen.

sauvignon blends

The blend of Sauvignon and Sémillon becomes a more equal one in traditional Bordeaux whites, where many of the best dry (and virtually all of the best sweet) whites are made from the partnership between grassy, taut Sauvignon and fatter, richer Sémillon.

Despite this description of Sémillon as weighty, it can lack flavour, zip, character, being a little blobby and ill-defined, or even thin and weedy. Sauvignon is a shot in the arm, character-wise. Interestingly, Sémillon is better suited to oak-ageing - *ergo*, wines that are a blend of Sauvignon and Sémillon such as the great Bordeaux whites, take to oak better than single varietal Sauvignons. Well, in my view, anyway. This is one of the greatest double acts in the world of wine: a white wine equivalent of a red made from a blend of Cabernet Sauvignon and Merlot, where the two components complement each other brilliantly, becoming, in the finest examples, more than the sum of their parts. Sauvignon Blanc is blended with Sémillon in wines from other parts of South West France – one of the most popular being white Bergerac.

Yet Sauvignon doesn't pair up so well with any other variety. You may come across examples of blends with Chardonnay from the New World which some wine-drinkers enjoy because they prefer the zest and aroma of pure Sauvignon mixed with something plumper. Personally, I would prefer to see these varieties kept apart. Australian Chardonnay stands up on its own, and Australian Sauvignon increasingly does, too. The best partner in Australia is, again, Semillon (spelled in the New World without the "é"), producing some impressive, well-balanced blends – above all in Margaret River, Western Australia. Usually, however, Sauvignon Blanc from the New World is encountered on its own.

Sauvignon has been grown in France for as long as anyone can remember. The Bordeaux and Loire Valley regions are its strongholds. Bordeaux is famous for its red grape Cabernet Sauvignon, while the Loire's best red is Cabernet Franc; these facts are relevant, because recent DNA tests have proven that both grapes are related to Sauvignon.

how sauvignon grew up

Long ago, it appears that Sauvignon Blanc was crossed with Cabernet Franc to produce Cabernet Sauvignon. Many wine-tasters will agree that there is a hint of "greenness" – a note of leafiness, even grassy, capsicum characteristics – in certain wines made from any of these three grape varieties.

Sancerre and Pouilly-Fumé (one hundred per cent Sauvignon Blanc, from the Loire Valley) became extremely fashionable around the world in the 1970s. This led to an increased respect for the variety in Bordeaux from the 1980s onwards. Modern vinification methods (rapid crushing shortly after harvesting, cool-temperature fermentation, and super-clean stainless-steel containers

in the winery) led to better wines all round. In California, a new style of Sauvignon was pioneered by Robert Mondavi, who oak-aged the wines a little and called them Fumé Blanc: a softer, sweeter-tasting style of Sauvignon that soon caught on, but is less popular today than it was in the 1980s. A better long-term fillip for Sauvignon came in the 1980s, when the New Zealand style arrived. What a wake-up call! The guides of twenty years ago barely mentioned these. Now Kiwi Sauvignon is one of the great New World classics. Sauvignon was redefined for many consumers – interestingly, just as the Loire Valley vogue slipped a little.

Many younger wine-lovers know the grape mainly as a supremely fruity, aromatic blast of gooseberry notes and perhaps a musky hint of cat's pee. Yes, cat's pee. It's there, in some wines, and it's not as bad as it sounds. A sign of just how well this applied to Sauvignon was the appearance, in the 1990s, of a label called "Cat's Pee on a Gooseberry Bush" in UK wine shops. Now the fruity, upfront but dry, unoaked style of Sauvignon is predominant around the world, and that includes parts of France and some wineries in California. Even so, many New World wines labelled Fumé Blanc are richer in style mainly because they are usually aged in barrel for a creamy, oaky finish – and sometimes they are a little sweeter.

Sauvignon might have slumped in popularity during the rise of New World Chardonnay in the late 1980s and '90s, but the Chardonnay backlash is now upon us, and Sauvignon Blanc, in unoaked form, is set to become even more popular over the next few years.

what will become
of sauvignon?

It's partly to do with quality, of course. Winemakers are facing up to the challenge of producing premium Sauvignon: in particular, focusing on the vineyard. Their wineries were modernized years ago, and stainless steel tanks gleam in the sun. Now, they are turning their attentions to viticulture and how to get the best out of the Sauvignon vine.

Mainly that has meant an increased trend towards canopy management: plucking off leaves, cutting back the vigorous growth in order to expose grapes to the sunshine and the fresh air. Riper, better-balanced Sauvignons should be the result. The use of clones of the vine that are especially designed to produce lower and better yields of grapes is another advance. In Chile, we should see better Sauvignon emerge as the vine is separated from the inferior Sauvignonasse growing in the vineyards. That said, there will always be boring, dull Sauvignon around, and if the grape does become more popular, its tendrils may spread into unsuitably hot or fertile vineyards. Watch out. Cool climates are the only way to go here, so choose wine from an area recommended in this book.

It will be interesting to watch the continued controversy over ageing. Sauvignon is not a great "ager", but now that a couple of decades of Marlborough Sauvignons are stacking up, some fascinating older wines are emerging that could change perceptions.

Finally, there is the subject of oak. We can expect little in the way of richly oak-aged Sauvignon, except in the case of the great Bordeaux whites. We will probably continue to see Sauvignons in which just a small proportion of the final blend has seen the inside of a barrel, but not much of the heavy oak of old-style Fumé Blanc.

the countries

It matters a great deal where a wine is made. The climate, the soil, the rainfall, the slope of the vineyard – all are crucial to the style of wine that results. As is the method of growing grapes, the winery equipment, even the character and ambitions of the winemakers in any one region. So the country of origin is an important key to understanding Sauvignon Blanc.

It doesn't matter how well Sauvignon Blanc performs abroad, France will always be its first home. This is where the vine first started producing great wine, around the Loire river and in the celebrated Bordeaux region. For many, France is still the source of the best and most elegant Sauvignons of all.

france

Top producers

(Some of these producers make blends of Sauvignon with other grape varieties; others make one hundred per cent Sauvignons.)

Henri Bourgeois
Lucien Crochet
Didier Dageneau
Pascal Jolivet
de Ladoucette
Alphonse Mellot
Vacheron
Vatan

Loire

France's Loire Valley is the source of some of the world's finest Sauvignon Blanc. The Loire river is the longest in France, rising near the centre of the country not far from the Rhône, and running north and west like a green gash all the way to the Atlantic Ocean, near Nantes. Along its banks, many different styles of wine are made.

The greatest Sauvignon Blancs are produced in the middle section of the river, in the heart of the country, southeast of Orléans. The most famous sources of wine here are Sancerre and Pouilly-Fumé. Many consider the

Sauvignons made in these two appellations to be the
best in the world.

Sancerre, in particular, defines the bone-dry, tangy,
mineral-clean style of the grape. There is a fresh perfume
and crisp flavour; expect lemon, grapefruit, fresh tart
gooseberry, and a hint of leafy, raw blackcurrant rather
than the richer lime, passion-fruit, and gooseberry-pie
of New World Sauvignon. Prices have risen in recent years,
and some Sancerres can be disappointingly bland, but
pick a good producer and a fine vintage and you should
get a concentrated, aromatic wine that is hard to beat
for zingily fresh, elegant, mouthwatering style. The best
areas have limestone-rich soils with some gravel and flint,
and it is possible to spot a hint of mineral and even
smoke in some wines.

In Pouilly-Fumé, that mineral-and-smoke character is
even more pronounced. Slightly further east, on the other
side of the Loire, Pouilly-Fumé's vineyards are particularly
prized around the town of St-Andelain, where there are
flint deposits in a type of soil known as silex. The word

Top producers

Sweet styles:
Château Climens
Château Suduiraut
Château d'Yquem

Dry styles:
Château Haut-Brion
Château La Louvière
Château Margaux
Château Smith-Haut-Lafitte
Domaine de Chevalier

fumé means smoked, as this soil gives a slightly smoky, gun-flint character to the wine – think of the aromatic wisp of grey after an old-fashioned pistol is fired. In reality, the wines are much like Sancerre and possibly less consistent.

Other good sources of fresh, crisp Sauvignon, sometimes with an extra-dry, almost chalky hint, come a little further east, from the villages of Menetou-Salon, Reuilly, and Quincy. Of these, Menetou-Salon is the best bet.

The prices of all the above wines have risen in recent years. For simpler, but less-expensive Sauvignon, look for Sauvignon de Touraine, from the area around the town of Tours. Chenin Blanc is the most important white grape grown here, but Sauvignon ripens well, too, producing tasty, everyday quaffing whites.

Then there are the Sauvignons made in the Loire region that are classified as Vin de Pays du Jardin de la France or "country wine from the garden of France". These are usually fresh, appealing, and straightforward wines, that, like Sauvignon de Touraine, need drinking while they are young and vibrant.

Bordeaux

Further southwest, Sauvignon comes into its own once
more around the city of Bordeaux, which is better known
for its red wines (often called claret in the UK) – now taking
up eighty-five per cent of production. White Bordeaux is
still important, however, and for the Sauvignon fan, a must.
It is usually made from a blend of Sauvignon Blanc and
Sémillon grapes (see "Blends", page 14), although more
pure (one hundred per cent) Sauvignons are now being
produced. Expect a grassy hint in most wines, and freshly
chopped lemon/lime fruit flavours.

Trade up from basic Bordeaux *blanc* and try the best of
Bergerac and the Côtes de Duras, plus more sophisticated,
sometimes fairly oaky, even powerful wines from Entre
Deux-Mers, Graves, and Pessac Léognan, which show how
complex and creamy white Bordeaux can be – at a price.

This is also the region where the great dessert wines
of Sauternes and Barsac are produced, again from a blend
of Sauvignon Blanc and Sémillon. These luscious sweet
wines are made from "nobly rotten" grapes: those which
have been affected by the botrytis mould, which causes

them to shrivel, concentrating their juices and sugar,
the finest wines taste delectable: of honey and apricots,
beeswax and dried candied peel, even roasted hazelnuts,
yet with a clean, tangy streak running through them.

Less expensive, less exciting, and often appealing
sweet wines are made in other areas near Bordeaux.
Côtes de Bergerac Moelleux (*moelleux* means "sweet")
is often seen, but Saussignac and Monbazillac are
especially recommended.

Other France

Outside the Loire Valley and the southwest, there isn't a
lot of Sauvignon Blanc grown in France; it is generally
too hot for this grape in the Rhône and the deep south
of France. That said, some Sauvignons are now appearing
from the Languedoc, labelled as Vin de Pays d'Oc. These
wines tend to be made in the rich, juicy New World style,
partly because the sun is so warm there that the grapes
naturally become riper than elsewhere in France, and partly
because the winemakers generally favour this very modern
style of white. Fine, these wines are reliably pleasant, and
a lot like the cheaper New Zealand and Australia offerings,
but don't expect any great subtlety or expression of
individual vineyard sites. You may come across a little
Sauvignon from Provence, although it's not very impressive
stuff. The only other French Sauvignon of note is
Sauvignon de St-Bris, from near Chablis, which makes
remarkably good, snappy, clean-tasting whites from this
grape. This area recently gained its own AC designation.

The AC system

The *appellation contrôlée*
(AC) system defines the
top category of French
wines according to their
origin. Wines from a
particular appellation
(defined on the bottle)
are made according to
regulations that specify
vineyard yields, grape
varieties, and production
methods. Although
officially the top-category
AC wines are not
guaranteed to be the
greatest, and some
disappointments are
inevitable. *Vin de pays*
("country wines") are also
regulated, although less
strictly than AC wines.
They do offer a
geographical definition
(eg. Vin de Pays d'Oc) and
are often labelled by the
grape variety. These can
be more exciting,
modern wines.

You will find Sauvignon from several areas of Italy, but as a rule, it is in the higher-altitude, northeastern parts of the country that the grape is at its best. In the mountainous sections near the borders of Austria and Solvenia, winemakers produce an aromatic, lean, mouthwatering Sauvignon that tastes pure, grassy, and crisp.

italy

Top producers

Edi Kante
Lageder
Lis Neris-Pecorari
Montanara
Niedermayr
Puiatti
Schiopetto
Tenuta dell'Ornellaia

The best wines are arguably from the prettily named Friuli-Venezia Giulia region in Italy's furthest northeastern nook. This area has been influenced by other countries' vines and wines, and today is known for its modern styles of dry white made from a wide range of varieties found in France, Germany, and Eastern Europe, as well as in Italy itself. It's a breezy region, swept through by cool mountain winds although protected by the northern peaks, with well-drained, hillside vineyards, sometimes carved into terraces.

Collio and Colli Orientali del Friuli are the specific parts of this region to visit for top Sauvignon. Here, there are plenty of smaller, quality-conscious producers, many of whom started producing impressive, mainly unoaked whites in the last fifty years – relative newcomers, then, by Italian standards. Sauvignon Blanc is made alongside Pinot Grigio, Chardonnay, and Pinot Bianco.

Further to the west, the neighbouring region of Trentino-Alto Adige also produces appealingly crisp, refreshing, if somewhat one-dimensional Sauvignon. This land of stunning mountain backdrops has a thriving tourist trade that laps up much of the decent white wine. A glass of local Sauvignon is a delight with fish from Lake Garda; in fact, the relatively light, northeastern Italian Sauvignon is extremely food-friendly, and washes down plenty of local cuisine effortlessly.

Elsewhere in Italy, several producers in Piemonte (northwest) are now creating attractive Sauvignons, richer in style than those found further east. A few winemakers have tried their luck in Tuscany, too, but further south the climate is simply too hot for this grape variety. Just a few wineries in Sicily and the south are experimenting with Sauvignon Blanc.

The DOC system

In Italy, DOC wines are those of controlled origin, from specific regions, made with specified grape varieties and to regulated styles – it's the equivalent of French AC (see page 27). DOCG indicates even stricter controls, but neither DOC nor DOCG guarantee top quality. IGT is the equivalent of *vin de pays*.

If the only Spanish white wine you've tasted has been traditional, heavily oaked, white Rioja, then it's hard to imagine a light, refreshing Spanish Sauvignon. But they do exist – mainly made in Rueda, close to Portugal's northeast corner. Part of the larger area known as Castile, Rueda produces the best Castilian whites.

spain

Top producers

Con Class
Hermanos Lurton
Marqués de Riscal

It wasn't always so. Rueda wasn't well-known for whites until late into the twentieth century. In fact, this far-flung, rural, rather old-fashioned part of Spain still seems quite sleepy. But since the 1970s, it has proved to Spanish wine drinkers around the world that it can produce modern, snappy, squeaky-clean whites, mainly using the local grape Verdejo and international star Sauvignon. The progressive Spanish *bodega* (winery) of Marqués de Riscal started it all over thirty years ago, by planting Sauvignon vines in sandy,

chalky, occasionally gravel-strewn soils. Now several highly reliable producers are turning out Sauvignon that tastes typically of grapefruit zest and lime: very moreish and great value to boot. Most is unoaked, although a few richer, creamier, barrel-aged examples have been spotted. Look for the word *Crianza* on the label, which means "oak-aged".

Little Sauvignon is grown in other parts of Spain. A few plantings exist on the far northern Basque coast, in two little-known wine regions called Chacolí de Guetaria and Chacolí de Vizcaya, but you'd have to go there to sample these obscure, tart wines. The Sauvignon vines are really being planted as an experiment, as they are not traditional in these regions.

The same goes for Costers del Segre, further east near Barcelona, where Sauvignon has been planted recently, along with other grapes new to the region. Currently, it is not permitted in DO wines of the region. Some Sauvignon is also grown in Penedès, an area better known for its *cava* and Chardonnay, and in Ribera del Guadiana, much further south near the Portuguese border.

The DO system

In Spain, DO wines are those of controlled origin, from specific regions, made with specified grape varieties and to regulated styles – it's the equivalent of French AC (see page 27). DOCa indicates even stricter controls, but neither DO nor DOCa guarantee top quality. *Crianza*, *Reserva*, and *Gran Reserva* indicate oak ageing.

Sauvignon Blanc lovers can pick up some tasty, well-priced wines from Central and Eastern Europe, but do be careful, as quality is patchy. Although there are plenty of great-value, deliciously modern wines available, particularly from Hungary, there are plenty of tired and faulty bottles, too. Understanding a bit more about this part of the winemaking world should help you pick a winner.

central & eastern europe

Hungary is still perhaps better known for its old-fashioned, meaty red wines, particularly Bull's Blood. And under Soviet rule, during the 1970s and 1980s in particular, its wineries did not keep up with the rest of the world, with the inevitable consequence that standards seriously slipped. That said, the country's wines are now enjoying a revival; modern techniques have arrived, talented winemakers are working hard, and the results can be attractive varietals, including Sauvignon Blanc. Hungarian Sauvignon tends to be dry, pungent, and savoury in character, sometimes even boasting a whiff of smoky bacon mingled with crisp, citrus-peel aromas. The areas of Hungary now making palatable Sauvignon include Mór, Aszár-Neszmély, and Etyek, all to the north of the country, and the best wineries around Lake Balaton, to the southwest.

In Bulgaria, you need to tread even more carefully. There are significant plantings of Sauvignon but few good wines have emerged – which is particularly disappointing as, back in the mid-1990s, it looked as though this country might start making plenty of good glugging whites. For now, however, Bulgarian reds and Chardonnays are looking better than its aromatic whites, too many of which taste oxidized and flat. You may be lucky and find a rare gem, however. The same goes for Romania; you may be fortunate with Sauvignon here, but it's a risky way to part with your money.

Sauvignon Blanc is also planted in Slovenia and Moldova but, as yet, the wines haven't made a regular appearance on the world stage. Development is painfully slow – which is understandable for countries that have seen so much upheaval of late. Watch out, though, decent Sauvignon from these corners of Eastern Europe should arrive one day.

Look out for

Some of Eastern Europe's more attractive whites appear under own-label in supermarkets. These wines can be great value for money.

Austrian white wines can be most impressive: racy and clean, with firm acidity, a real wake-up call to the senses. Sure, the country turns out premium oaky Chardonnay, but who doesn't? Austria's aromatic, dry whites made from Riesling, Sauvignon Blanc, and local grape Grüner Veltliner are much more exciting – especially for those with jaded palates.

the rest of europe

Most of the best Sauvignon in Austria comes from the region of Styria, in the far south of the country, near the border with Slovenia. Here Sauvignon is quite a specialty, and it is consistently high-quality: expect a bracingly dry, mouthwatering style with hints of lemon, lime, and grapefruit, and something of the stony, mineral character found in the Loire. A few richer, oaked examples can be unearthed. The best part of Styria for Sauvignon is known as the Südsteiermark, the southernmost part.

Some equally appealing Sauvignon can be found outside the Styrian border, especially in the Wachau wine region further north, near Krems. This all sounds great, but bear in mind that prices are high for Austrian wines. They almost always come from small "boutique" wineries so there are no economies of scale.

Drinkable Greek wine seems to be finding an international market at last. Winemakers use a mix of internationally known and obscure local grape varieties. Sauvignon doesn't crop up a lot, but it has been found in salty, dry, crisp whites as part of a blend and occasionally on its own in an oaked "fumé" style. Look for more in the future as modern Greek winemaking finds its feet. Although it's nice to see a focus on unusual local vines, most consumers will want to see the well-known grapes in there, too, so Sauvignon's future seems assured.

Talking of the export market, if you see a young Sauvignon Blanc from Portugal packaged in a modern bottle, chances are it has been made by a canny winemaker with an eye on the main game overseas. It will almost certainly be palatable and clean. Just be aware that the warm climate here is not particularly suitable for Sauvignon, and Portugal has many more interesting table wines to offer. There are tiny plantings of Sauvignon in other European countries (Germany, where it is known as Muskat-Silvaner; Luxembourg; Switzerland; and England), but the wines are rare as hen's teeth.

Top producers

Austria: Lenz Moser
Pichler
Polz
Willi Sattler
Stiegelmar
Manfred Tement

Greece:
Domaine Kostas Lazaridis
Tsantalis

Portugal: Fuiza Bright

Say "Australian white wine" to most people and they automatically think of Chardonnay. Push them a bit harder and the Semillon grape (again with no "é") might come to mind. But they won't picture Sauvignon Blanc, and that's not surprising. Until recently, hardly any enjoyable Sauvignons were made in Oz: probably only two or three at most. In fact, very few were made at all, and most of these were rather fat, oily, and overblown. No competition for the New Zealanders, then.

australia

Of course, the huge success of New Zealand Sauvignon was almost certainly one of the reasons why the Aussies didn't bother that much with this grape variety. Another was that they were already enjoying plenty of success with other grapes (yes, Chardonnay, and to a lesser extent, Semillon and Riesling). A more sensible reason was the climate. It's too hot by far in many Aussie winemaking regions to create the sort of zesty, crisp, aromatic Sauvignons that are so well-loved around the world. But these days, any serious wine-producing country wants to master all the great grapes, and Australia is now a very serious wine producer indeed. Inevitably, some winemakers are determined to conquer Sauvignon, and are showing some degree of success. A number of the Sauvignons planted in cooler, fresher spots such as the Adelaide Hills (South Australia, east of Adelaide city), Tasmania, and parts of Victoria are now convincingly crisp and elegant, yet fruit-driven with a gooseberry/citrus-fruit tang. Tasmania produces the most subtle, French-style Sauvignon Blancs, refreshingly different from the Australian blockbuster-style of white that can get a bit tiresome.

Some of the boutique wineries at Margaret River, south of Perth in Western Australia, make more rounded, complex, but well-balanced Sauvignon, mainly blended with Semillon in a style that conjures up lime peel, oranges, and angelica. This is a lovely way to enjoy Sauvignon – although not the cheapest. Margaret River blends seem to age well and they are consummately food-friendly.

Is Australian Sauvignon here to stay? Yes. It has become a valid wine style, although it will never eclipse Australian Chardonnay or Semillon, and neither will it ever really frighten the Kiwis.

Top producers

Cape Mentelle
Cullen
Delatite
Katnook (including the Riddoch label)
Knappstein Lenswood
Nepenthe
Pipers Brook
Shaw & Smith

It's not often that a brand-new wine-growing region takes on the established classics and appears to beat them at their own game. But that's what happened in the 1980s, when the cool, sunny, stony-soiled area of Marlborough, on New Zealand's South Island, began coming up with Sauvignon Blanc to upstage the traditional whites of the Loire and Bordeaux.

new zealand

In reality, it's impossible to argue that, stylistically, New Zealand's Sauvignons are "better" than those of France, as they are quite different. Marlborough Sauvignon is unique.

It's almost a shocking wine. It hits the senses with a blast of ripe, baked gooseberry pie, lime juice, tomato vines, and grapefruit. Riper, richer examples seem packed with asparagus, passion-fruit, sweaty notes (male armpits!), and savoury, catty hints; more subtle examples have freshly chopped green grass creeping in; under-ripe ones head towards green bell pepper (capsicum), herbs, nettles, blackcurrant leaf. You get the picture: New Zealand Sauvignon ain't subtle. If you had to pick one of those startling nuances to define it, it would be that gooseberry, singing out, pure and bright, just as all the best New Zealand wines sing out with a clean, clear, fruity note.

It's hardly surprising that many wine-drinkers around the globe were dazzled by this thrilling new style of

Top producers

Marlborough: Cloudy Bay
Hunter's
Isabel Estate
Jackson Estate
Lawson's Dry Hills
Seresin
Vavasour
Villa Maria
Wither Hills

Sauvignon, that arrived just as we were getting a shade bored with restrained (for which read "disappointingly bland") European whites. But in truth, New Zealand Sauvignon can get tiring, too. It *is* a bit relentless: that ripe, in-yer-face, fruity/aromatic character.

And so the arguments rage on as to which are the best Sauvignons of all: Old World or New, Loire or Marlborough. Both are valid, of course. The Loire certainly has the edge for elegance, but the New Zealanders have forced a lot more expression out of this grape variety than anyone before or since. True fans of Sauvignon Blanc should find a place in their hearts and cellars for both types.

The astonishing success story of New Zealand Sauvignon Blanc really only began in the 1970s, when the first vines were planted in Marlborough. At the time, the area was chosen partly because land was cheap; little did the first pioneers know that a whole new style of white wine was about to emerge, though it's nice to think a few true visionaries had a hunch. After all, the land was highly promising, with its well-drained, gravel soils full of large stones (which reflect the sun's heat). Its climate, too, was perfect for fine, aromatic whites, with bright sunny days, cool nights (to help preserve high acidity), and an unusually long, slow ripening season that gradually coaxes the vines into producing concentrated flavours and aromas.

Yet there can be problems in Marlborough, especially if the grapes don't get ripe enough, or if they become too ripe and produce flabby wines. So the quality of its Sauvignon does vary from year to year – more so, in fact,

Top producers

Hawke's Bay: Craggy Range Sacred Hill

Canterbury: Giesen Pegasus Bay

Central Otago: Mount Difficulty

Nelson: Neudorf

Martinborough: Palliser Estate

than a lot of other New World wines. But in general, this scenic but sleepy rural backwater, once populated only by sheep, now produces a true New World classic, and it has been transformed, in just thirty years, into one of the most exciting wine regions in the world, mainly due to Sauvignon Blanc.

Marlborough connoisseurs will be interested to know that there are two distinct parts of the region. The main Wairau Valley plains, where most of the big-name wineries are, and an even stonier spot called the Awatere Valley to the south, where savoury, concentrated styles (not hugely different) are made along with some admirable reds.

Several Marlborough labels have become well-known to wine buffs, but only one is world-famous: Cloudy Bay. The classic Cloudy Bay style is rich and rounded, with a little Semillon and barrel-ageing adding weight and body. It remains a great wine, but it is expensive, and other top Sauvignons now rival it (see top producers and page 54). Try several other labels to compare and contrast them if you are lucky enough to drink Cloudy Bay regularly. And try other aromatic whites from New Zealand to get a better perspective on this country's wines – although there's little to touch the exciting Sauvignons.

Do try Sauvignon Blanc from other parts of New Zealand. Still on the South Island, bottles from cool-climate Canterbury, further south around the city of Christchurch, are more minerally and restrained than their Marlborough cousins. The Waipara subregion is where the best wines are appearing. Further north, a handful of producers in

Nelson is giving the bigwigs in neighbouring Marlborough
a run for their money with sophisticated wines, while
on the North Island (where the weather is warmer, more
humid, and consequentially less suitable for this grape),
there is one important region for Sauvignon. That's
Wairarapa, around the town of Martinborough, near the
south coast. Sauvignons from this area are a must if you
like New Zealand whites; they are relatively rich and
rounded on the palate, but slightly less brash and
outspoken than Marlborough examples. Expect plenty of
ripe gooseberry flavours, but with more rounded, creamy
edges rather than that explosion of tanginess that marks
out the famous South Island style.

Finally, just one or two worthy Sauvignons are made in
deeply trendy (and stunningly beautiful) Central Otago on
the South Island, and in Hawke's Bay, a warm area on the
North Island that is much more famous for reds.

If those great winemakers, the Australians, have struggled with Sauvignon, then so have the Californians. Or rather, other people haven't always taken to the California style of Sauvignon which, in general, is more rich, fat, and oaky, and less crisp, grassy, and refreshing than most Europeans want. "Flabby" is the way its detractors describe Californian "Fumé Blanc", which is what the traditional West Coast oaked styles are called (*fumé* means smoked – *see* page 24).

north america

That said, some of the best Californian Fumé Blancs have always been impressive, as long as they have enough acidity to keep them at least a little fresh and zesty. The worst are indeed flabby: poor wines made from over-cropped fruit grown in too hot spots, then over-oaked so that the lovely clean fruit is overwhelmed. The good news is that the number of poor ones seems to be diminishing; growers don't get paid an awful lot for Sauvignon grapes, so if they are not interested in the variety, they can't be bothered any more.

And a new style is emerging, more in line with other New World Sauvignons, with gooseberry, citrus fruit, and grass to the fore. There still aren't a lot of these wines around, but there are enough to prove that it can be done. This recent success is due to a small band of Sauvignon enthusiasts using cooler-climate sites, taking more care in the vineyard, lowering yields, and generally being more meticulous. Still, Sauvignon will never be the most popular grape grown here, and I suspect the battle over Sauvignon styles (and whether it is worth bothering to take this variety entirely seriously) will continue to rage for quite some time.

If Sauvignon isn't the Californian winemakers' favourite grape, then it certainly isn't top of the charts in Oregon or Washington. A little Washington Sauvignon exists, and like all the best wines here, it can have a deliciously pure, fruity note. But Chardonnay and, to some extent, Semillon are taken more seriously, and plantings of Sauvignon are in decline. Similarly, in Canada, a few excellent Sauvignons are made, although other varieties (Riesling, Chardonnay) are considered more important. Which is a shame. Is it too much to hope that North America will take Sauvignon more seriously in the future?

Top producers

California: Caymus
Chalk Hill
Frog's Leap
Kenwood
Matanzas Creek
Mondavi
Sanford

Washington State:
Hogue

Will the real Sauvignon please stand up? In Chile, it can be hard to tell when a white wine is made from Sauvignon Blanc and when it is made from a look-alike variety called Sauvignonasse. At least when the wines are young. Sauvignonasse (aka Sauvignon Vert) does not stand the test of time, and its wines lose their fresh streak of acidity quickly, fading and growing dull. Until very recently, the Chileans had been convinced that all they had was Sauvignon Blanc. Now they know that a lot of these plantings are, in fact, the inferior grape. Some vineyards are a jumble of the two, so you just end up with a blend of both in your glass. Not ideal, then.

south america

In general, only Sauvignons from new vineyards (mid-1990s onwards) are pure, and it's impossible to tell from a label which wines have been made from them. But, future improvements are expected as more pure (one hundred per cent) Sauvignon Blanc is produced. If you do get a good, genuine Sauvignon from Chile, it will be pleasantly crisp and highly aromatic, with an emphasis on green-fruit flavours (lime, gooseberry, hint of pear) and often some grassiness. The most impressive come from fairly new vineyards in the cool Casablanca Valley, close to Valparaiso on the coast. This sandy-soiled, breezy, maritime area is arguably Chile's best white wine region, and although Chardonnay is more widely planted there, the Sauvignons from Casablanca are superbly perfumed, tangy, and elegant. You may come across Sauvignon Blanc made in Argentina, a country that is experimenting with this variety along with numerous others. As yet, a specific style has not emerged and the Argentinians seem more interested in Chardonnay and Viognier.

Sauvignon is also made in Uruguay, and the one or two that have come my way have been perfectly palatable. However, Uruguay is only just emerging as a player on the international stage and is concentrating on its red wines.

Top producers

Chile: Echeverría
Mont Gras
San Pedro (including 35 South label)
Villard
Viña Casablanca

Last, but by no means least in our round-the-world tour of
Sauvignon sources, we come to South Africa and the spectacularly
beautiful vineyards of the Western Cape. Here, the wines have
improved no end over the past five to ten years. This is since a
new post-apartheid generation took over, better vineyards
came on stream, and modern methods hit the wineries.

south africa

Consumers who have been disappointed by the standard
of Cape wine in the past should take a new look, and not
just at those well-known Stellenbosch reds. The quality
of the white wines has suddenly leapt up and Sauvignon
Blanc is one of the most exciting varieties to feature in
the new era of Cape wines.

Indeed, South Africa could now accurately be described
as the third great producer of Sauvignon Blanc, along with
the Loire and New Zealand. The best wines hit an appealing
balance somewhere between the rich aroma and ripe,

vibrant fruit of Marlborough and the more elegant, mineral-and-grass French style.

A lot of Cape Sauvignons are undoubtedly fruity, with fresh passion-fruit, gooseberry, and citrus-fruit flavours, but they are not overwhelming or pungent, and there is a crisp, mineral note in evidence, too, so these wines trip-off-the-tongue easily and refreshingly. In case this all sounds too good to be true, there are also some mundane, mediocre Sauvignons produced here, as anywhere – but not many. The cheapest Cape Sauvignons can be too simple, with a slightly confected pear-drops flavour, but, in general, the quality is running high, and winemakers are enthusiastic about making premium wines from the grape.

The best regions for Sauvignon are also beginning to emerge. Unsurprisingly, they are the cooler spots that do not suffer from South Africa's sudden bursts of heat. Vineyards cooled by the ocean breezes off False Bay are better than those which bake in the sun. Constantia, on the coast close to the Cape Town suburbs and, interestingly, where the Cape's first vineyards were established by Simon

Top producers

Bouchard-Finlayson
Buitenverwachting
Klein Constantia
Mooiplas
Neil Ellis
Springfield Estate
Steenberg
Thelema
Vergelegen
Villiera

van der Stel in 1685, is making an impressive crop of wines, with that passion-fruit note to the fore. The area of Walker Bay/Elgin, a low-temperature spot southeast of Cape Town, is another interesting source of elegant, somewhat grassy, even steely wine, while the winemakers of the pretty valley of Franschhoek turn out decent Sauvignon Blanc by planting at slightly higher altitudes on the slopes.

All of which perhaps makes it a surprise to learn that Robertson, a much warmer, arid inland region, has become renowned for its Sauvignons (as well as its Chardonnays). Robertson, however, is blessed with rare, rocky, limestone soils that stress the vines and produce intensely flavoured, well-balanced whites. Robertson Sauvignon, with its distinctly mineral, almost chalky appeal, and zesty lemon fruit, is almost French in style. Look for the odd Sauvignon from other Cape regions, too – Swartland, Tulbagh, even cool hilly corners of Stellenbosch.

All in all, exciting times in the Cape. If you think the Chenin Blancs and Colombards produced here are boring (and much of the time, you'd be right), and you tire of the often very rich, oaky South African Chardonnays, then do give the Sauvignons a whirl.

FLAGSTONE

FREE RUN
SAUVIGNON BLANC
2001

buying, storing, & serving

Now you know where the important Sauvignons are sourced and the different styles that can be produced. The next stage is buying a bottle, so here is the lowdown on shopping for Sauvignon, plus some tips on whether to store it or quaff it, how to serve it and which dishes to match with it.

Whether or not you think Sauvignon Blanc is good value for money depends on your enthusiasm for it. Of course, this is true of all wines, but perhaps especially so in the case of Sauvignon. A lot of wine-lovers complain that it's one-dimensional – crisp and refreshing, but not much more – and they baulk at paying the high prices demanded for top labels.

quality vs price

It is also argued that, while grapes such as Chardonnay and Riesling can be multi-layered and deeply fascinating, Sauvignon never achieves such complexity, and thus should never cost a fortune.

Champions of Sauvignon counter that they occasionally come across brilliant wines that entirely deserve their high price tags. We claim top Sauvignons are every bit as exciting as other fine whites. You are likely to find good Sauvignon Blancs from the Loire that *are* worth splashing out on. And, incidentally, their prices are not way out of reach; a lot of other wines will set you back much more.

Admittedly, these gems are rare. The answer? Tread carefully, choose a reputable producer, and keep an eye out for the best vintages. It might help to know that Sancerre is generally a little more reliable than the others. The Loire Valley's Sauvignon de Touraine is much cheaper and often great value as an everyday quaffer. Vin de Pays du Jardin de la France is another bargain. Further south, Bordeaux and the southwest in general, are more patchy in terms of value for money. For every decent bottle of basic Bordeaux *blanc*, Entre-Deux-Mers, and Graves, there are several dull, commercial blends. Trade up to better-quality, more expensive, often oak-aged, Bordeaux whites.

What about New Zealand's Sauvignons? The price of some of the most famous have become scary, especially for the most illustrious names. Yet if you want to show off with a famous label from New Zealand, go ahead (but watch out for ludicrous mark-ups in restaurants for these wines). That said, it is well worth trying other, lesser-known labels from Marlborough, in particular; some of the less-glitzy, less-fussed-over Sauvignons are excellent, and are giving the star wineries a serious run for their money.

Elsewhere, South Africa is impressing with its superb value-for-money wines, this time higher up at the mid- to premium-end of the market. If you enjoy New Zealand's wines, then give the slightly cheaper ones from the Cape a whirl. A little cheaper still, Chile is producing a number of good Sauvignons in the middle price bracket. Yet it's hard to beat Hungary for bargain Sauvignon, if you like the savoury, aromatic style and a very low price tag.

The great dessert wines of Bordeaux (blends of Sauvignon and Sémillon) are justly expensive. Very little is made and everyone wants it: a simple case of supply and demand pushing up the price. For a cheaper, somewhat less complex version, try the luscious Monbazillac.

PRODUCT C

SANC

APPELLATION SANC

Le Comte

20(

Like the dry, crisp, refreshing style of Sauvignon (á la Loire Valley)? Well, there plenty of other racy whites around that are well worth trying. Pick young, fresh, zesty German Riesling for a start: more mouthwatering citrus-fruit and mineral flavours, this time with an apple and floral note to boot. Go for a *Trocken* style if you like a dry edge. Still in Germany, sample wines made from the Scheurebe grape, which has a distinctive grapefruit flavour. These are quite rare, but look hard and you'll find a few exports.

other wines to try

Riesling from Austria is another good bet for the Sauvignon-lover: extremely fresh, clean, and dry. And while you're trying Austrian wine, don't miss a grape variety called Grüner Veltliner, which has a peppery, almost spicy edge, but again, lots of wake-me-up, zingy, citrus fruit. Then there's Alsace, home of France's most unusual and exotic white wines, almost all of which are unoaked. Sauvignon-lovers will enjoy the easy-going, food-friendly Pinot Blancs and grapey, gluggable Muscats in particular.

If you prefer the fruity, vibrant, pungent Kiwi style of Sauvignon Blanc, then take a look at young New World Semillon. It hasn't got the same blast of gooseberry and asparagus, but it is grassy, aromatic, and smoky when it's first made (if you allow it to age in the bottle it turns honeyed and rich and mellow).

Simple party plonk in the cheap-and-cheerful style of basic, crisp Sauvignon (*i.c.* refreshing, but with little personality) can also be found in France's South West wines made from Colombard and/or Ugni Blanc. Even better, try the pleasantly limey, laid-back Chenin Blancs of South Africa – perfect for washing down party grub!

As for sweet wines, it's fair to say that there's nothing quite like the great French dessert wines of Bordeaux, made with a blend of Sauvignon Blanc and Sémillon. It's a safe bet to say that if you love these, you will probably enjoy other sweet wines that combine firm acidity, luscious sweetness, and the beeswax richness of noble rot. Try the majestic Tokáji of Hungary, Australian botrytized Semillon, sweet German Riesling, and Austrian stickies from the Neusiedlersee region.

And is it too fanciful to suggest that that if you like the leafy, grassy quality of Sauvignon Blanc, then you might head for reds that show the same quality? We have already seen that Sauvignon is related to Cabernet Franc, the red grape primarily known for its important role in France's Loire Valley. Wines made from Cabernet Franc typically taste leafy – like a brush through green currant bushes, and they can carry a whiff of green pepper (capsicum), too.

The Sauvignon-lover's first stop for reds should probably be a Loire Valley Cabernet Franc.

Most Sauvignon Blanc is released young and is
designed to be enjoyed in its first year, while
the wine is vibrant, fresh, and singing with fresh
fruit flavours, or even a slight tartness. The cheap,
basic wines will start to fade after this time,
losing that lively character and tasting dull.
They are simply not built to last. Drink 'em up!

when to serve

For lots of people, that's exactly how *all* one hundred per
cent Sauvignon should be consumed: pretty quickly after
it appears on the shop shelves. It's certainly true to say
that Sauvignon is not a great "ager", for it isn't a wine
to be cellared away for years in order to reach its peak.
However, the more concentrated and well-made wines
do last surprisingly well.

Try an older (good-quality) Sauvignon from New Zealand
and you'll discover a more mellow but still delicious,
rich wine into which all sorts of interesting nuances
have begun to creep: coffee beans, lime marmalade,
tinned asparagus.

In Bordeaux, there's less argument. The fine, oaked
Sauvignon/Sémillon dry whites, that is, can benefit a
great deal from a couple of years in the cellar, losing any
hard edges, or rawness, or sawdusty oak, and becoming
better knit and more balanced as a result. Don't overdo

it, though, or you'll end up with a tired old white. The wonderful dessert wines can be left to rot (sorry!) for longer. Over time, expect the tangy apricot and citrus-peel flavours to mellow and grow honeyed, even beeswaxy, with more unctuousness and a richer colour. The character of dried peel, nuts, chocolate, coffee – even faint hints of mushroom and toast – might start to creep in. Twenty years and more is quite all right – if unusual these days – to keep a good Sauvignon dessert wine.

Which occasions suit Sauvignon Blanc best? If you were to divide white wines into "cold weather" and "hot weather" styles, then Sauvignon suits hot weather better. It's a mouthwatering, pithy, wake-up-the-palate grape variety, as opposed to, say, Chardonnay, which often makes rich, oaky comfort whites for indoor dinner parties. Crack open cold, frosty bottles of dry Sauvignon at *al fresco* parties, on hot balmy evenings, after dusty journeys, or on picnics – any occasion where instant refreshment is needed. It makes a great aperitif, a reasonably light lunchtime wine, and a perfect match for salads and other summery food.

It is *not* perhaps the best wine to bring out with Christmas lunch and all the trimmings, or on a freezing cold day after a long walk. Sauvignon isn't meant to warm your heart in the sense that rich, hearty wines are – it's meant to tickle your palate and conjure up sense of green, leafy Spring.

One very important rule: Sauvignon Blanc should be served chilled. Always. There isn't a single Sauvignon or Sauvignon blend, dry or sweet, that doesn't taste crisper, more refreshing, more thirst-quenching, more tangy, more inviting all round when it's cold. Not icy cold, mind. There's something about extremely cold white wine that is somehow closed and muted because of its almost-frozen state. Let the character shine through, then, but do give it a chill – about two to three hours in the fridge should do it. And once it has been opened, keep it cold. Too many wines start off cold and end up at room temperature by the time you finish drinking. If you're in a restaurant, ask for an ice bucket.

how to serve

Sauvignon Blanc is not a great keeper as far as wine ageing goes. The same is true of its life once the bottle has been opened. Some hearty, powerful wines can last for up to a week after opening, but Sauvignon is relatively fragile, and should be drunk within two days of pulling out the cork. Always re-seal the bottle after opening to help slow down the oxidation process, and store it in a cool, dark spot. The fridge is perfect, but a warm kitchen windowsill is not.

There are plenty of fancy, faceted, or coloured glasses around and they won't harm your wine at all. Plastic cups can smell a little odd, but you can swig it straight from the bottle if you like! The perfect way to savour Sauvignon is to serve it in glasses that are, ideally, plain (so you can see the wine's colour), with long stems (so your fingers rest there, instead of warming the wine around the bowl) and medium-sized, perhaps with a tapering top so the aroma is concentrated a little. Fill the glasses only half-way up or less, and top up regularly. That way, your wine stays cool and fresh, and it also helps when you come to sip it. You can swirl the wine around as you raise it to your mouth, releasing the remarkable aroma of the wine.

Sauvignon Blanc is often served as an aperitif because of its light fruitiness, crisp acidity, and dryness. Fine. The only problem with this is that you might miss out on the fact that Sauvignon is also extremely versatile as a partner for food. It makes a great match for fish dishes, working like a squeeze of fresh lemon and lime.

what to serve with

Try riper New World examples with rich white fish, juicy scallops, sweet-tasting crabmeat – even salty tinned tuna. Pair lighter European ones with delicate, plainly grilled sole or plaice. Even mildly spicy fish dishes (Thai fish recipes, kedgeree or Indian prawn curries) go well with this grape variety, though do avoid anything oaky with fish unless the fish is smoked, in which case go right ahead.

Sauvignon is great news if you happen to be vegetarian, as it matches plenty of vegetable and salad dishes, even apparently difficult ones such as asparagus, tomato salad, or dressed leafy salads. Why? It's all because of its high acidity (good with the sourness of tomatoes, the vinegar in the dressing), and the uncluttered, unoaked character of most Sauvignons. Try a chilled, straightforward Sauvignon Blanc with rich, cheese-topped vegetable bakes, too – vegetable lasagne, baked aubergines, even cheese fondue or melted cheese on toast – the crisp wine cuts through the oily flavour brilliantly. Talking of cheese, Sancerre is still the best match for goat's cheese (but most European Sauvignon is good, too). Sauvignon is also one of the few wines that washes down chicken curry well; it doesn't exactly enhance the food, but neither does it clash. Finally, don't miss a fine sweet blend – Sauternes or Barsac – with dessert. My favourite matches are with a good tarte tatin or other fine appley dessert, or with creamy dishes. And try these fine sweet wines with salty, soft blue cheese (Roquefort) and rich, creamy pâtés, too.

index

AC system (France) 26
acidity 62
Adelaide Hills 10, 37
ageing 17, 19, 31, 42, 58
Alsace 56
Argentina 47
aroma 10, 11, 12, 17, 61
  for aromas to be expected
  from particular regions see
  those regions
Auckland 41
Australia 10, 15, 36-7, 57
Austria 34, 56, 57
Awatere Valley 42

Barsac 25, 63
Bergerac 15, 25
Bordeaux 13, 14, 16, 19, 25-
  7, 55, 57-58, 63
  sweet/dessert wines 25-6,
  57, 59, 63
Bordeaux Blanc 55
Botrytis cinerea 8, 25-7
botrytized Semillon 57
boutique wineries 34, 37
Bulgaria 32-33
buying wine 53-8

Cabernet Franc grape 16
Cabernet Sauvignon grape
  16
Cabernet Sauvignon/Merlot
  blends 15
California 13, 16-17, 44-5
Canada 45
canopy management 18
Canterbury 41, 42
Casablanca Valley 46-7
cellaring 58-9
Central and Eastern Europe
  32-3
Central Otago 41, 43
Chardonnay 8, 15, 29, 34,
  36, 45, 47, 54
  Sauvignon Blanc blends
  15
Chenin Blanc 24, 57
Chile 18, 46-7, 55
climate 10-11, 19, 21
  for climates in particular
  regions see those regions
clones 18

Cloudy Bay 14, 42
Colombard grape 57
Côtes de Bergerac Moelleux
  27
Côtes de Duras 25

Dessert wines
  Bordeaux 25-7, 55, 57, 58
  see also sweet wines
DO and DOC system (Italy)
  29
DO(Ca) system (Spain) 31

England 35
Entre-Deux-Mers 25, 55

Flavour 8, 9, 12, 13, 17
  for flavours expected from
  particular regions see
  those regions
food, to accompany wine 29,
  62-3
France 10, 16, 17, 22-7
  see also wine growing
  areas by name
Fumé Blanc 17, 19, 44

Germany 35, 56, 57
glasses 61
grapes 8-9
Graves 25, 55
Greece 34-5
growing localities 10-11
Grüner Veltliner grape 34, 56

Hawke's Bay 41, 43
Hungary 32-3, 55, 57

Italy 10, 28-9

Languedoc 8, 26
Loire Valley 10, 11, 12, 16,
  17, 22-4, 41, 54-5, 58
Luxembourg 35

Margaret River 15, 37
Marlborough 10, 11, 17, 19,
  38-43, 55
Marqués de Riscal 30
Martinborough 43
Menetou-Salon 24
methoxypyrazines 8
Moldova 33
Monbazillac 26, 55
Mondavi, Robert 16-17

Müller-Thurgau grape 12
Muscat 56
Muskat-Silvaner grape 35

Nelson 41, 43
New World wines 7, 15, 17,
  23, 26, 42, 45, 56, 62
  see also under individual
  "New World" areas
New Zealand 10, 11, 12, 17,
  36, 38-43, 55, 58
noble rot 8, 25-7, 57
North America 44-5
  see also California

Oak 13, 17, 18, 19, 29, 31,
  35, 55, 56, 58
Oregon 45
over-cropping 12
oxidation 60

Pinot Bianco 29
Pinot Blanc 56
Pinot Grigio 29
Portugal 35
Pouilly-Fumé 11, 16, 22, 23
price and quality 54-5
Provence 27

Quincy 24

Restaurant price mark-ups
  55
Reuilly 24
Rhône valley 27
Riesling grape 34, 36, 45, 54
  alternative to Sauvignon
  56
  sweet wines 57
Rioja 30
ripening 9, 10, 13, 18, 24
Robert Mondavi 16-17
Robertson region 11, 50
Romania 33
Rueda 30

St-Andelain 23
Sancerre 11, 16, 22-3, 54, 63
Saussignac 27
Sauternes 25, 63
Sauvignon Blanc grape 10-
  13, 16-19
  blends 14-15, 25, 35, 37,
  55, 57, 63
  the future of 18-19

Sauvignon de St-Bris 26
Sauvignon de Touraine 24, 54
Sauvignon Jaune 17
Sauvignon Vert 46
Sauvignonasse grape 18, 46
Scheurebe grape 56
Sémillon (Semillon) grape
  36, 45, 56
  botrytized 57
Sémillon/Sauvignon Blanc
  blends 14-15, 25, 37, 42,
  55, 57, 58-9
serving wine 60-3
Sicily 29
Slovenia 33
soil 11, 12
  for soils in particular
  regions see those regions
South Africa 9, 48-50, 55, 57
South America 46-7
  see also Chile
Spain 30-1
stainless-steel tanks 16, 18
Stel, Simon van der 49-50
storing wine 58-9, 60
supermarket (own-label)
  wines 33
sweet wines 25-7, 57, 63
  see also dessert wines
Switzerland 35

Tasmania 10, 37
terroir see climate; soil
Tokaji 57

Ugni Blanc grape 12, 57
Uruguay 47

Verdejo grape 30
vinification see winemaking
vin de pays 27
Vin de Pays d'Oc 27
Vin de Pays du Jardin de la
  France 24, 55
Viognier grape 47
viticulture 18

Waipara 42-3
Wairarapa 43
Wairau Valley plains 42
Washington State 45
winemaking 12-13, 16-17,
  18, 27

Yields, value of low yields 12